A Guide for Using

Stuart Little

in the Classroom

Based on the novel written by E. B. White

This guide written by **Lorraine Kujawa**

Teacher Created Resources, Inc.
6421 Industry Way
Westminster, CA 92683
www.teachercreated.com

ISBN: 978-1-57690-628-6

©2000 Teacher Created Resources, Inc.
Reprinted, 2008
Made in U.S.A.

Edited by
Leasha Taggart

Illustrated by
Ken Tunell

Cover Art by
Wendy Chang

Table of Contents

Introduction

A good book can touch our lives like a good friend can. It can stimulate our minds and imaginations and inspire us in ways we never realized. With a good book we are constantly in good company and never bored. It can give us a story to cherish in our hearts forever.

In *Literature Units,* we have chosen books that are sure to become treasured friends for life.

Teachers using this unit will find the following features to supplement their own valuable ideas:

- Sample Lesson Plans

- Pre-reading Activities

- A Biographical Sketch and Picture of the Author

- A Book Summary

- Vocabulary Lists and Suggested Vocabulary Activities

- Chapters grouped for study with each section including the following:

    —*quizzes*

    —*hands-on projects*

    —*cooperative learning activities*

    —*cross-curriculum connections*

    —*extensions into the reader's own life*

- Post-reading Activities

- Book Report Ideas

- Culminating Activities

- Research Activities

- Three Different Options for Unit Tests

- Bibliography of Related Reading

- Answer Key

We are confident that this unit will be of great value to your lesson planning. Through the use of our ideas, we hope that your students will increase their knowledge and enjoyment of literature and find new literature "friends."

Sample Lesson Plans

Each of the lesson plans suggested below can take from one to several days to complete.

Lesson 1
- Introduce and complete some or all of the pre-reading activities (page 5).
- Complete the "New York City—The Big Apple" activity (page 6).
- Read "About the Author" with your class (page 7).
- Read the book summary with your students (page 8).
- Introduce Section 1 vocabulary (page 9).

Lesson 2
- Read Chapters 1 through 3. Review the vocabulary words and discuss their meanings in the context of the story.
- Complete a vocabulary activity (page 10).
- Introduce and do "Telling Fiction from Real Life" (page 13).
- Learn about animals in literature (page 14).
- Practice drawing a mouse (page 12).
- Work on meeting challenges (page 15).
- Administer Section 1 "Quiz Time" (page 11).
- Introduce the vocabulary list for Section 2 (page 9).

Lesson 3
- Read Chapters 4 through 6. Review the vocabulary words and discuss their meanings in the context of the story.
- Do a vocabulary activity (page 10).
- Work on "Sailing Ships" (page 17).
- Complete "What Did You Say?" (page 18).
- Work on the New York map (page 19).
- Consider some adventures people have had (page 20).
- Administer Section 2 "Quiz Time" (page 16).
- Introduce the vocabulary list for Section 3 (page 9).

Lesson 4
- Read Chapters 7 through 9. Review the vocabulary words and discuss their meanings in the context of the story.
- Do a vocabulary activity (page 10).
- Build your own catboat (page 22).
- Discuss animals that swim (page 23).

- Write letters to dog trainers (page 24).
- Work on training a pet (page 25).
- Administer Section 3 "Quiz Time" (page 21).
- Introduce the vocabulary list for Section 4 (page 9).

Lesson 5
- Read Chapters 10 through 12. Review the vocabulary words and discuss their meanings in the context of the story.
- Do a vocabulary activity (page 10).
- Construct an action car ride (page 27).
- Learn about cats (page 28).
- Create some clever quotes (page 29).
- Discuss rules (page 30).
- Administer Section 4 "Quiz Time" (page 26).
- Introduce the vocabulary list for Section 5 (page 9).

Lesson 6
- Read Chapters 13 through 15. Review the vocabulary words and discuss their meanings in the context of the story.
- Do a vocabulary activity (page 10).
- Create Ames' Crossing (page 32).
- Develop flags and messages (page 33).
- Explore types of sailboats (page 34).
- Decide what you would do (page 35).
- Administer Section 5 "Quiz Time" (page 31).

Lesson 7
- Discuss questions your students have about the story (page 36).
- Assign book reports and research activities (pages 37 and 38).
- Begin work on one or more culminating activities (pages 39–42).

Lesson 8
- Administer Unit Test: 1, 2, and/or 3 (pages 43–45).
- Discuss the test answers and possibilities.
- Discuss the students' enjoyment of the book.
- Provide a list of related reading for students (page 46).

Before the Book

Before you begin to read *Stuart Little* with your students, do some pre-reading activities to stimulate interest and enhance comprehension.

1. What does the title of this book tell students about the main character, and how do they think it might become important in the story?

2. Find out what the students know about New York City and list their responses on a poster. Then do some research on New York City through the Internet, encyclopedias, and people who have been to or lived in New York City. Note your information on your poster.

3. What do students watch on TV that might be considered fantasy? What do they watch that might be considered reality? How can one tell the difference?

4. Ask students these questions.

Differences

— How do people you know react when they meet someone very different from themselves?
— How do you react?
— How does it feel to be different from the others in a group?
— Does being different change the way you would behave?

Sailing:

— Have you ever been sailing?
— How is sailing different from boating?
— What would you need to know as a sailor?
— Would you like to sail a sailboat?

Adventure:

— Do you like adventure?
— If you could have any adventure you wanted, what would it be?
— What items would you need to have for this adventure?
— Of what would you need to know to survive your adventure?
— Draw a picture of yourself on your adventure. Share it with the class.

Before the Book *(cont.)*

New York City—The Big Apple

The story of *Stuart Little* takes place in New York City. New York City is often referred to as the Big Apple.

There are many interesting things to see and do in New York City. Below is a list of some of them. Check off the ones you would like to visit or do in New York City.

When you have finished your checklist, share it with the class. Look up some of the places listed to find out more about them before you make your choices.

_____   The Statue of Liberty

_____   Ellis Island

_____   South Street Seaport

_____   Staten Island Ferry

_____   New York Stock Exchange

_____   Federal Reserve

_____   Greenwich Village

_____   Chinatown

_____   Little Italy

_____   Rockefeller Center

_____   Radio City Music Hall

_____   Carnegie Hall

_____   The Museum of Modern Art

_____   AT&T's Info Quest Center

_____   Gallery of Science and Arts

_____   Saint Patrick's Cathedral

_____   Central Park:

    _____   Zoo

    _____   Horseback riding

    _____   Ice skating

    _____   Feeding the pigeons and squirrels

    _____   Sailboating

    _____   Riding in a horse-drawn carriage around the park

_____   Metropolitan Museum

_____   Guggenheim Museum

_____   Empire State Building

_____   Madison Square Garden

Share with the class what you know about New York City and why it might be called the Big Apple.

About the Author

Born on July 11, 1899, in Mount Vernon, New York, Elwyn Brooks White—or E. B. White, as he has become known, grew up believing in the adventure of the imagination and the spirit.

The son of a piano manufacturer, E. B. White graduated from Cornell University in 1921 and began working for the *New York Magazine*. He also worked as a reporter for the *Seattle Times* and *Harper's Magazine* and was a part of the U.S. Army from 1938 to 1943.

Of the 18 or so books that White has written, the stories that are remembered most fondly are his children's books: *Stuart Little,* written in 1945; *Charlotte's Web,* written in 1952; and *The Trumpet of the Swan,* written in 1970.

Many readers have asked if White's stories are true. His answer was this, "They are imaginary tales . . . real life is only one kind of life—there is also the life of the imagination."

These imaginary stories came to White from everyday experiences. Once, on a long train trip from New York City to Virginia, White dreamed of a small creature with the looks of a mouse who was "nicely dressed, courageous, and questing." So began *Stuart Little.*

While living in the country, White became acquainted with many animals that lived on his farm. He found it extremely unfair that the animals trusted him, not knowing that he would betray them in the end. White especially enjoyed the pigs and began to think of a story that would find a way to "save a pig."

As White was thinking of a hero for his story about a pig, he became interested in spiders. He enjoyed watching them so much that when it was time to go back to the city, White carefully snipped an egg case from a web he found. He carried it in his suitcase back to New York City, where the eggs hatched in his sock drawer. White once said, "Spiders are skillful, amusing, and useful." This is how *Charlotte's Web* began.

White's children's books have won many awards throughout the years. *Charlotte's Web* accepted four book awards including a Newbery Honor Book in 1953 and the Lewis Carroll Shelf Award in 1958. *The Trumpet of the Swan* received seven nominations and awards that included the National Book Award in 1971, as well as the Laura Ingalls Wilder Medal in 1970 for a "substantial and lasting contribution to literature for children." In 1971 White won the National Medal for Literature.

E. B. White passed away on October 1, 1985, but his delight and love of animals lives on in the imaginative tales he has woven for us.

Stuart Little

by E. B. White

(HarperCollins Publishers, Inc. 1945, 1973)
(Available in Canada and UK, HarperCollins Publishers Ltd.; AUS, HarperCollins)

When Stuart is born into the Little family, they become aware that he looks very much like a mouse. It is very unusual that regular people like the Littles have a mouse for a son, but no one becomes very excited about it.

Mr. and Mrs. Little and Stuart's older brother George love Stuart and make many accommodations for Stuart's size. Two of the problems the Little family face are setting up a bed for such a small person and making clothes small enough for him to wear. Stuart needs a ladder to get up to the washbasin and uses a hammer to open the faucet. His father runs a long string so Stuart can turn on the bathroom light.

Stuart, however, is very helpful around the house. He goes down the bathtub drain to retrieve his mother's ring, finds Ping-pong balls that have rolled under the furniture, and helps his brother George play the piano by unsticking one of the hammers inside the piano while George plays.

Because Stuart is a mouse and so small, he is not well liked by Snowbell, the family cat. When Stuart tries to show off his muscles to Snowbell, he manages to roll himself up in the window shade. Snowbell tries to mislead the family into thinking that Stuart has gone down a mousehole, and they believe it until Stuart is unrolled from the shade by his brother George. Stuart seeks out many adventures. He rides a bus to Central Park, sails a schooner in a race, and even becomes locked in a refrigerator.

While recovering from bronchitis, Stuart meets Margalo, a lovely bird that the Littles have rescued. They become fast friends, and Margalo becomes a guest of the family and resides in the Boston fern in the Littles' living room.

On one of his outings, Stuart becomes trapped in a garbage truck and finds himself facing danger on a barge in the East River. He is saved by Margalo, however, and is safely transported home.

When springtime arrives, Margalo becomes the object of a plan by Snowbell and a white Persian cat. A local pigeon intercedes, and the frightened Margalo takes flight.

Stuart is heartbroken and decides to leave home in search of Margalo. The first stop Stuart makes on his venture is to see Dr. Carey, whose sailboat Stuart raced. The doctor lends Stuart a small car for his travels.

Stuart befriends a school superintendent and becomes a substitute teacher for a day. He meets Harriet, a young lady his size, and asks her to go boating with him. When he finds his boat has been ruined, Stuart becomes unhappy. Harriet tries to get Stuart to be more optimistic but leaves when she cannot succeed in making him happier.

Stuart again heads north in search of Margalo, the bird that comes "from fields once tall with wheat, from pastures deep in fern and thistle."

Vocabulary Lists

On this page you will find the vocabulary lists that match each sectional grouping of chapters as outlined in the Table of Contents (page 2). Activities to reinforce the vocabulary words can be found on page 10 of this book.

Section 1: *Chapters 1–3*

whiskers	cane	belittling	louse	washbasin
clothespins	unsuitable	worsted	hauled	handkerchief
embarrass	pantry	curious	moisten	carpet sweeper
solemnly	crouch	radiators	faucet	

Section 2: *Chapters 4–6*

custom	trapeze	disgust	snatched	shipshape
suitable	budge	sobbed	spectacles	gleaming
vigorous	chuckled	gait	conductor	aboard
wedged	occupied	trouser	enormous	

Section 3: *Chapters 7–9*

serge	barometer	collision	penetrate	peering
rigging	shivered	halyards	broth	scow
fragments	flotsam	daring	dwell	buoys
consternation	ominous	tapioca	hoisted	tugs

Section 4: *Chapters 10–12*

delicatessen	pariah	jauntily	stalked	scholars	nix
obliged	bureau	streamlined	nimbly	reminiscently
coop	crept	rhinestones	appropriately	abomination

Section 5: *Chapters 13–15*

sarsaparilla	tranquil	cranky	dandelion	rank
ruinous	moss	stamen	souvenir	lacing
trifle	swindled	ballasted	astern	carnival

Vocabulary Activities

1. Make a **Picture Dictionary** in your classroom. Using 3" x 5" (8 cm x 13 cm) cards, write one of the vocabulary words at the top of each card. After looking up the word, use the rest of the space to draw a picture showing the meaning of the word. Post the students' pictures in the hall, on a bulletin board, or on a large sheet of butcher paper. Discuss the meanings of the words. Invite others to view your Picture Dictionary.

2. Play **Vocabulary Charades.** After students have looked up the vocabulary words assigned, call on one student to act out one of the vocabulary words in front of the class. The others may have the vocabulary list in front of them. The student who guesses correctly has the next chance to act out another word. Encourage students to plan their charades ahead of time. Vocabulary words can also be assigned to each student.

3. Play the game of **Match Up.** Without having looked up the vocabulary words beforehand, give students cards to wear that have either the vocabulary word or the meaning of the word. Have students walk around the room trying to match up the meaning with the vocabulary word on it. Use a timer and set a time limit. The class can then go over the meanings of all the words together.

4. Create a **Crossword Puzzle.** Make copies of the vocabulary words with each letter in a one-inch block on graph paper. Run off copies for the students. In teams of two, have students cut out words and paste them onto a large sheet of paper to form a crossword puzzle. All touching letters must make a word. The group with the most words used wins. Set a time limit.

5. Make a **Spring Vocabulary Bouquet.** Cut out a stencil of a tulip large enough to clearly print a vocabulary word up the stem. Have students use the stencil to make enough tulips using colored paper for each of their vocabulary words. Write the meaning of the word or a sentence using the word inside the tulip. Display each bouquet on construction paper and hang them in the classroom.

6. Design a **Vocabulary Bulletin Board.** Develop a bulletin board displaying mouseholes. Each mousehole is to have the definition of a vocabulary word on it. Have cutouts of mice at the bottom of the bulletin board with a vocabulary word on each. Have students pin mice to their correct mouse holes.

7. Create a **Stained Glass Vocabulary Window.** Pass out 4" x 2" (10 cm x 5 cm) plastic film to each student. Have students print clearly one of their vocabulary words with a colored marker. Tape to a window to give a stained glass effect as a reminder of their new words.

8. Make a **Vocabulary Clock.** Write vocabulary words on 3" x 4" (8 cm x 10 cm) sentence strips. Cut out and place words over the numbers on the clock in the room. Use the words to tell time. You can also place words next to the daily schedule on the board and use the words instead of the time.

9. Play **Vocabulary Hopscotch.** On several 8½" x 11" (22 cm x 28 cm) pieces of poster board, print the definition of each vocabulary word. Line up the poster boards on the floor in the shape of a hopscotch game. Have students toss a small bean bag onto one of the definitions. After reading the definition, the student must say the word it defines. You may have teams or play individually with a limited number of tosses. Laminate definitions for longer wear.

Quiz Time

Directions: Answer the following questions about Chapters 1, 2, and 3 of *Stuart Little*.

1. What difficulties did the Littles face when they found out Stuart was a mouse?

    _____

    _____

    _____

2. Why was the doctor called for Stuart?

    _____

    _____

3. Give an example of how you could tell that Stuart's parents were kind people?

    _____

    _____

4. How did Stuart meet the challenges of being smaller than everyone else in his house?

    _____

    _____

5. Was Stuart afraid of danger? What did he do that showed his courage?

    _____

    _____

    _____

6. Name three things Stuart did that an ordinary boy could not possibly do?

    _____

    _____

7. What poems did Stuart's parents not want Stuart to hear?

    _____

    _____

8. What did Stuart do once he was up in the morning?

    _____

    _____

9. What did George, Stuart's brother, try to do to help Stuart?

    _____

    _____

10. What invention could you think of that would help Stuart around the house? Use the back of this sheet to draw your invention.

Drawing a Mouse

The mouse in *Stuart Little* was drawn in a way that gives Stuart human-like qualities. Follow the directions below to create both a realistic version and a more imaginative version of a mouse. Consider what Garth Williams, the illustrator of *Stuart Little*, might create.

Realistic Mouse

A. Draw seven ovals for the body shape. Add a tail. Make circles and ovals for the leg and paws.

B. Outline the body. When satisfied, go over the shape in pen or thin marker and erase inside the pencil lines.

C. Add eyes and whiskers.

D. Add a nose and texture for the fur, ears, hair, and shadows.

Imaginary Mouse

A. Draw two circles for the body and one circle for the head. Add ears and a nose as shown.

B. Add three ovals for each arm, and three for each leg.

C. Outline, connecting all parts. Erase the interior lines. Draw clothes, as well as eyes, a nose, and whiskers. Outline in pen or thin marker and erase inside marks.

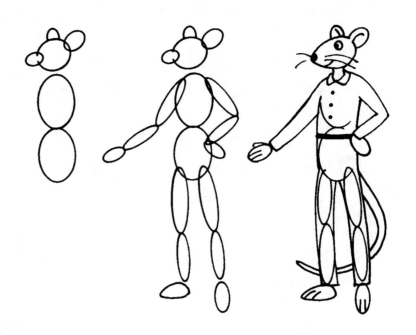

Telling Fiction from Real Life

E. B. White, the author of *Stuart Little*, once said, "Real life is only one kind of life—there is also the life of the imagination." Knowing the difference between the life of the imagination and real life is important because we live our everyday time in real life; however, it is often fun to enjoy the life of the imagination, too.

Below are several situations that might take place in real life or the life of the imagination. In groups of three, look at these situations and place a check in the correct column to indicate whether the situation is real or from the imagination.

	Real	Fiction
1. A newspaper provides weather predictions.		
2. A boy flies home after school.		
3. A girl dances on top of a pumpkin.		
4. Water flows from a bottle and never stops.		
5. The ocean has living creatures in it.		
6. A mouse sings in a play.		
7. A meatball falls from a plate and bounces out the window.		
8. You can ride a horse across the United States.		
9. A girl races a train and wins the race.		
10. Some people can run faster than a bicycle.		
11. Three dogs write to the President of the United States.		
12. Children write books for their library.		
13. You can read a book with 1,000 pages in it.		
14. After school, the teacher eats and sleeps in the cafeteria.		
15. People can see in a room with the lights turned out.		
16. At night, birds change into bats.		
17. There are birds that can talk.		
18. An apple will float in water.		
19. A child can swim across the water.		
20. Some dogs can understand French.		

Choose one of these situations and write a story about it on the back of this paper. Include three parts in your story:

- the introduction of the characters and the situation
- the event that happens to create a problem
- the solution to the problem that was created

After you have proofread your story and rewritten it, read it to your classmates and have them decide if it is real or fiction.

Animals in Literature

Many animals, like the mouse in *Stuart Little*, have been used to tell stories to children and adults. Discuss as a group animals used in books to tell a story. Below is a place for you to record your findings.

Name of Animal	Type of Animal	Name of Book

Extra Information

Use an encyclopedia, books, or the computer, to find out these facts about one of the animals in your list above. Use the lines below to list the following:

Name of animal_____

Its size _____

Where it lives _____

What it eats _____

How many babies it might have at one time _____

What kind of coat it has _____

Its color _____

Type of feet it has _____

Does it lay eggs or are its babies born alive?_____

Two interesting facts you learned _____

_____

Meeting a Challenge

Stuart found challenges in many of the activities in which he participated. He and his family met these challenges with the use of their imaginations. Below is a list of challenges that the Little family faced. In a small group, discuss what the family did to meet each challenge. Write your reflection on the lines at the right.

1. Stuart was too small to wear regular clothes.

2. Mrs. Little was worried that Stuart would hear children's stories and be frightened.

3. Stuart could not reach the washbasin.

4. Stuart was unable to open the faucet to wash up.

5. When George played the piano, one key always stuck.

1. _____
   _____
2. _____
   _____
3. _____
   _____
4. _____
   _____
5. _____
   _____

In this section, your job is to clearly imagine three challenges that you may encounter in real life and at least two different ways to meet each challenge.

Challenges	Possible Reactions	Possible Reactions
1. _____	1. _____ _____	1. _____ _____
2. _____	2. _____ _____	2. _____ _____
3. _____	3. _____ _____	3. _____ _____

Lastly, each student in your group can speak with an older student or adult in your school or at home and ask them to explain a challenge they faced in their lives and how they met that challenge. Record their responses below.

Get together with your group and discuss ways each person you interviewed met his or her challenge. Find a way they could have dealt with it differently and place that in the box at the far right. Share your ideas with the class.

Challenges	How the Person Reacted	Other Possible Reactions
1. _____	1. _____ _____ _____	1. _____ _____ _____
2. _____	2. _____ _____ _____	2. _____ _____ _____

Quiz Time

Directions: Answer the following questions about Chapters 4, 5, and 6 of *Stuart Little*.

1. How did Stuart get rolled up in a shade?

    _____

    _____

2. What did Snowbell say when Stuart flew up into the shade? Use quotation marks.

    _____

    _____

3. What did Snowbell do to mislead Stuart's parents about where Stuart was?

    _____

    _____

4. What did George want to do to find Stuart?

    _____

    _____

5. How was Stuart rescued?

    _____

    _____

6. What did Stuart mean when he said, "As for my hat and cane being found at the entrance to the mousehole, you can draw your own conclusions."?

    _____

    _____

7. Why didn't Stuart carry an ordinary dime to ride the bus?

    _____

    _____

8. List at least five of the sailing terms Stuart used.

    _____

    _____

9. Why was this chapter called "A Fair Breeze"?

    _____

    _____

10. In what ways did Stuart seem very sure of himself?

    _____

    _____

Sailing Ships

Stuart enjoyed sailing Mr. Carey's schooner at Central Park's pond. Stuart seemed to know a great deal about sailboats. You can also learn about sailboats. The terms below tell about different parts of a sailboat. Read the definitions of the words and place the word on a line by the part of the boat it identifies. You may color the sailboat when you finish. Also, add the water, sky, and some land for a background.

hull—the body of the sailboat
bow—the front of the boat
stern—the rear of the boat
boom—pole at right angle to the mast that holds the sail straight
keel (centerboard)—a board extending into the water for balance
rudder—a fin that steers the boat
tiller—a handle for the rudder
spar (mast)—pole that holds the sail
sail—sheet of cloth to catch the wind
jib—the smallest sail
rigging—ropes or lines

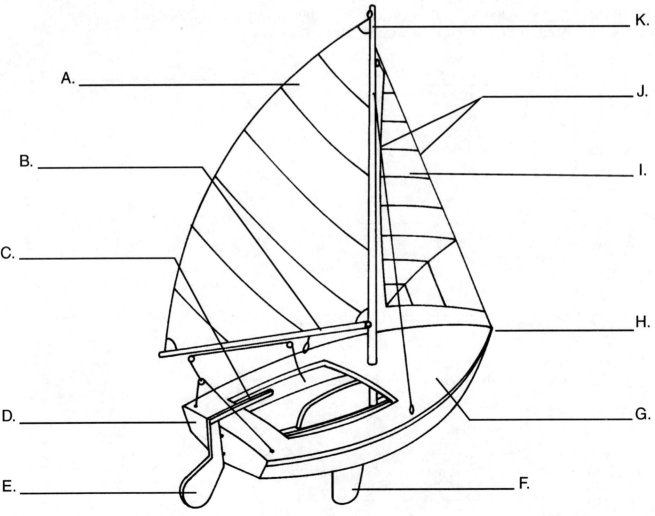

What Did You Say?

Stuart and the other characters in the book often used expressions that were unusual and interesting. Below are some of those expressions.

With a partner, discuss what you think these expressions might mean.

_____ 1. "Live and learn" (Stuart–chapter 6)

_____ 2. "Holy mackerel!" (Snowbell–chapter 4)

_____ 3. "Just don't get yourself all worked up." (Mr. Little-chapter 5)

_____ 4. "Well, for the love of Pete" (George–chapter 5)

_____ 5. "I beg pardon." (conductor–chapter 6)

_____ 6. "Bravo!" (man–chapter 6)

_____ 7. "Foul means!" (man–chapter 6)

_____ 8. "By the by" (man–chapter 6)

_____ 9. "Bon voyage." (man–chapter 6)

_____ 10. "I take all I can get." (Stuart–chapter 4)

A. Excuse me.

B. Try to stay calm.

C. You are not fair.

D. I try as hard as I can.

E. The older you are, the more you know.

F. Just a minute.

G. I am surprised!

H. Have a good trip.

I. I am amazed!

J. Congratulations; good job.

When you are finished looking at the quotes from the book, try your hand at explaining these expressions. Write what you think these sayings are telling you.

1. A stitch in time saves nine.

_____

2. Beat the clock.

_____

3. Today is the first day of the rest of your life.

_____

4. Even Steven.

_____

5. Hop to it.

_____

6. Try to buy some time.

_____

7. It's not over 'til it's over.

_____

8. Early to bed, early to rise makes a man healthy, wealthy, and wise.

_____

9. Time flies when you're having fun.

_____

10. Don't count your chickens before they've hatched.

_____

New York, New York!

Stuart Little found New York an interesting place to live. See what you can find out about this large city.

- Find New York City on a map of New York state.

- Is it an island? _____ What is an island? _____

- In what section of New York state is New York City? (N, S, E, or W) _____

- What is the population of New York City? _____

Using the map below, your library, the Internet, or any textbooks available, find out five interesting facts about New York City. Include places of interest to see, people who live there, transportation, recreation, etc., and follow the directions for making a poster of New York illustrating your impressions of that city.

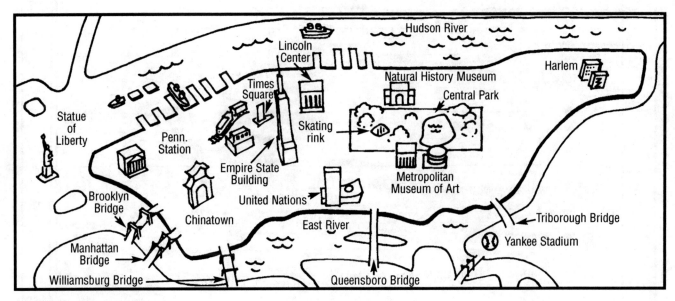

Making a Poster

In partners or small groups, gather these materials:

- five 3" x 5" (8 cm x 13 cm) cards
- paste
- large poster board
- paintbrush
- scissors
- colored construction paper
- poster paint
- pencils

1. Cut out large letters from construction paper to spell New York City. Paste them across the top of your poster board.

2. On the poster board, draw a large map with pictures of what you think the city of New York looks like, leaving room for five 3" x 5" (8 cm x 13 cm) cards.

3. Paint your poster.

4. Write a fact you learned about New York City on each of your cards.

5. When the paint is dry, paste your fact cards onto your poster and display it.

Adventures

Stuart had many adventures in his life. He was lowered into a drain, rolled up in a shade, and shipwrecked on a schooner. Many people have had adventures. In order to find out some enjoyable adventures that people have had, you need to ask them.

Interview people to find out if they have had an adventure. Good people to ask are firefighters, emergency helpers, nurses, doctors, and veterinarians. Sometimes there are people in your family or school who have had adventures they might like to share with you.

Ask them the following questions and record their answers below.

1. What was your most enjoyable adventure?

   _____

   _____

2. How did your adventure begin?

   _____

   _____

   _____

3. Who was involved in your story?

   _____

   _____

4. What happened that made it so exciting?

   _____

   _____

   _____

5. How did it end?

   _____

   _____

   _____

6. Ask them to draw a picture of their experience and sign it. Don't forget to thank them.

Quiz Time

Directions: Answer the following questions about Chapters 7, 8, and 9 of *Stuart Little*.

1. Describe how LeRoy, the owner of the *Lillian B. Womwrath*, looked and acted.

   _____

   _____

   _____

2. What accident happened at the shore, and how did it affect the race?

   _____

   _____

   _____

3. Briefly describe what occurred during the race.

   _____

   _____

   _____

4. What were some of the things Mrs. Little did after finding Stuart in the refrigerator?

   _____

   _____

5. How did each member of the family show Stuart he or she cared for Stuart while he was ill?

   _____

   _____

6. What did Stuart do to be kind to Margalo when he met her?

   _____

   _____

7. Stuart said, "I guess there's going to be something doing after all." Explain.

   _____

   _____

8. How was Margalo able to save Stuart from the East River?

   _____

   _____

9. What did Mrs. Little do to thank Margalo for saving Stuart?

   _____

   _____

10. Choose one of the characters in the story and explain what type of person you think he or she is. Give three examples to prove your point. Use the back of this sheet.

Building Your Own Catboat

Stuart and the people at Central Park had a great time sailing their sailboats. You can build a small sailboat, called a *catboat*, in your classroom. Gather the materials below and carefully read the directions. Check off each section as you complete it.

Materials

- crayons
- pencil
- glue or tape
- clay
- a straw
- paper towel
- 3" x 5" (8 cm x 13 cm) card
- string or dental floss
- scissors
- white cloth or white paper

Directions

1. Enlarge the patterns below. Before cutting out patterns, use a crayon to color both sides of the boat.

2. Cut out the boat pattern. Do not cut into the bottom of the boat, as this will create leaks.

3. Fold on the dashed lines and paste or tape the tabs so they overlap.

4. Press clay so it fits the bottom of the boat. With a pencil, outline the bottom of the boat onto the clay. Cut away excess clay with the edge of your 3" x 5" (8 cm x 13 cm) card. Lay clay inside the boat as a ballast (weight to keep the boat from tipping).

5. Cut out the sail pattern. Glue or tape the tab of the sail to the side of the straw, matching the tip of the sail to the tip of the straw. Let it dry completely.

6. Stand the straw and sail into the clay as shown. It may be necessary to add more clay to keep the sail standing.

7. Attach string to the end of the sail with glue, tape, or a small slit in the top of the straw. When dry, press the other end of string into the clay.

Congratulations! You are ready to set sail.

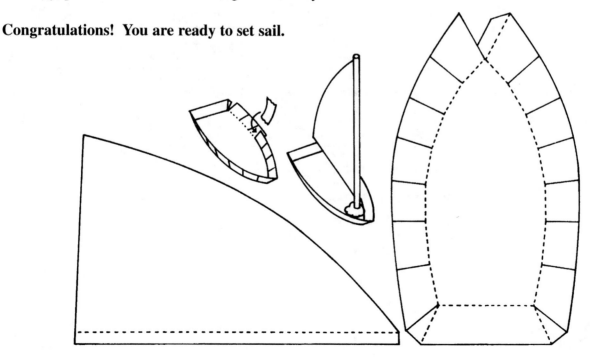

Animals That Swim

When Stuart fell into the pond in Central Park, many people thought he would drown. Surprisingly, Stuart knew how to swim. Many animals that we don't think of as swimmers can swim.

With a partner, list ten animals that live on land. Use the chart below. Research together to find out which animals can swim and which cannot. Record your findings on the chart across from the animal's name.

	Name of Animal	Swims	Doesn't Swim
1.			
2.			
3.			
4.			
5.			
6.			
7.			
8.			
9.			
10.			

Look for other interesting facts about the animals you have looked up and write the information in the box below.

Letters to Dog Trainers

Stuart could help his brother George and his parents with many things around the house. Margalo helped Stuart. The pigeon helped Margalo. Many animals are helpful. Some of the most helpful animals are dogs.

Dogs often help the blind, people with hearing problems, police officers, and firefighters. They even pull dog sleds. Use the sample letter and envelope below to write a letter and ask for information on dog training.

(your address)
(date)

Dear _____,

Our _____ grade class is studying how dogs are trained to work with people. I am interested in information about _____ dogs. Could you please send me any information you have on this subject? Thank you for your time.

Sincerely,

(your name)

---

your address

their address

Below are the addresses of people who train dogs:

National Association of Dog Obedience Instructors
P.O. Box 432
Landing, NJ 07850-0432

United States Police Canine Association
5091 Washington Rd.
Delrey Beach, FL 33484

International Federation of Sleddog Sports
7118 N. Beehive Rd.
Pocatello, ID 83201

Guide Dogs for the Blind, Inc.
P.O. Box 151200
San Rafael, CA 94915-1200

American Greyhound Track Operators
1065 NE 125th St., Suite 219
North Miami, FL 33161-5832

Assistance Dogs International
10175 Wheeler Rd.
Central Point, OR 97502

Training a Pet

Stuart, George, Mr. Little, Mrs. Little, Snowbell, and Margalo all lived together peacefully. Pets can live well with people, but there are things people need to do to train a pet in order to live with them happily. Some of the pets that can be trained to live with people are dogs, cats, horses, ants, snakes, birds, fish, and hamsters.

To find out how to train a pet, we can go to a pet store, a book, the Internet, or other people for information.

- Choose a pet you have or would like to have, and research some ways of training your pet.

- In the space below, write about four things you would like to train your pet to do.

- Tell how you are going to "kindly" train your pet.

- Tell from where or from whom you got your information.

Type of Pet _____

_____

_____

_____

_____

_____

_____

_____

_____

_____

_____

_____

Quiz Time

Directions: Answer the following questions about Chapters 10, 11, and 12 of *Stuart Little*.

1. What kind of influence did the Angora cat have on Snowbell?

   _____

   _____

2. Why did the pigeon feel that she needed to warn Margalo?

   _____

   _____

3. What effect did the note from the pigeon have on Margalo?

   _____

   _____

4. Why did the pigeon write a note rather than speak to Margalo?

   _____

   _____

5. What did Stuart wrap up to take on his journey with him?

   _____

   _____

6. Why did Edward Clydesdale speak so strangely: "How 'oo oo, Soo'rt"?

   _____

   _____

7. Dr. Carey said that his patient had a "sound idea" about looking in Central Park for Margalo. Tell a "sound idea" you have heard or shared with someone.

   _____

   _____

   _____

8. What was Stuart's idea for maintaining discipline?

   _____

   _____

9. What did Stuart decide to teach the day he was a substitute?

   _____

   _____

10. If you were Chairman of the World, what would you consider important?

    _____

    _____

Action Car Ride

Stuart borrowed Dr. Carey's car for his journey while in search of Margalo. Below are outlines of Stuart and the car he drove. On cardstock or index paper, reproduce the cutouts on this page so you will have two copies for each student.

1. Carefully cut out the squares on this sheet and the second sheet. It is very important that the sides are cut evenly.

2. Place them in order with both #1s together, followed by both #2s, etc.

3. Staple on the left side of the pack, making sure all sides are evenly lined up.

4. Flip through your pack and view Stuart's ride in Dr. Carey's car.

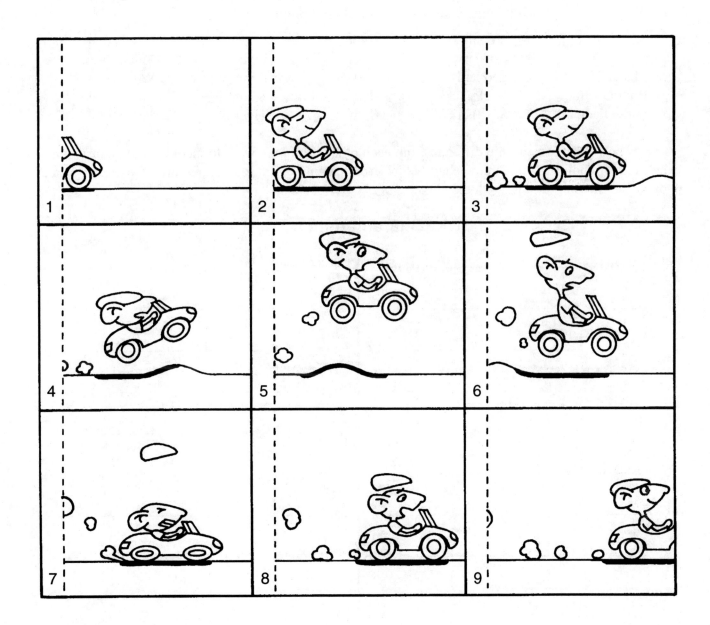

Cats

Chapter 10 of *Stuart Little* mentions cats in several places. Each of the cats in the story is found in a different location. Look through the chapter with a partner and find the six cats mentioned and where they live. List each in the chart below. Share your chart with the class when you are finished.

	1	2	3	4	5	6
Cats						
Where They Live?						

There are many types of cats in the world today. With your partner, research two of the cats below by searching on your computer, in the encyclopedia, or in the library.

Abyssinian	Somali	Calico	Cheetah	Egyptian Mau
Jaguar	Bobcat	Lion	Lynx	Maine Coon
Manx	Leopard	Persian	Puma	Rex
Russian Blue	Ocelot	Serval	Siamese	Silver Tabby
Snow Leopard	Scottish Fold	Sphynx	Tiger	Turkish Cat

Describe how your two cats are different from each other. You may want to include color, hair length, voice, size, friendliness, etc., in the chart below. You may also want to get a picture of your cat from a book or the Internet to share with the class.

Characteristics

Cat #1 Name _____   Cat #2 Name _____

1. _____

   _____

2. _____

   _____

3. _____

   _____

4. _____

   _____

1. _____

   _____

2. _____

   _____

3. _____

   _____

4. _____

   _____

Clever Quotes

In *Stuart Little,* much of the plot and details of the story depend on conversations between the characters. These are called quotes, and they are emphasized by quotation marks. When the pigeon says, "Well, the old thing!", we know she is talking because of the quotation marks. The rest of the writing tells us what is happening in the story.

In the sentences below, write what you think the characters would say. Choose words that make sense and place them between the quotation marks.

1. The boy reached for his glove on the baseball field and felt his feet sink into the mud.
   "_____," he cried.

2. Mary began crossing the cool stream in her bare feet. She looked back at her cousin and said,
   "_____."

3. Pulling on the sail was all Stuart could do as the boat tilted sideways.
   "_____" he said.

4. Riding an elephant was fun. Josh leaned over and called out, "_____
   _____," into the elephant's ear.

5. Yolanda crawled under the house to be alone and listen to her parents talking overhead.
   "_____" she heard them say
   through the floorboards.

Now it's your turn. Below and on the back of this paper, write a short story of your own. Use at least five quotes of your own to make your story interesting and fun. Remember to use quotation marks.

_____

_____

_____

_____

_____

_____

_____

_____

Rules, Rules, Rules

When Stuart was a substitute teacher for a day at School #7, he taught a lesson on rules. There are different rules for different places. Perhaps a rule in the classroom, "No running," for example, is not a good rule in the gym. Rules should make sense. There should be a reason for each rule. Below is a chart that has room for eight good rules for several places (cafeteria, home, bus, store, movie theater, etc.). Record them on the left. Decide for yourself or discuss with an adult why each rule is important, and then write why it is on the right.

Rule	Where?	Why?
1.		
2.		
3.		
4.		
5.		
6.		
7.		
8.		

Quiz Time

Directions: Answer the following questions about Chapters 13, 14, and 15 of *Stuart Little*.

1. Who did the storekeeper say Stuart should meet? Why?

   _____

   _____

2. Why was the town where Stuart met Harriet called Ames' Crossing?

   _____

   _____

3. Why did the storekeeper say, "It's a nice canoe," when Stuart asked if it leaked?

   _____

   _____

4. Why was it a good or bad idea for Stuart to imagine exactly how his meeting with Harriet would turn out?

   _____

   _____

5. Why did Stuart worry about the letter?

   _____

   _____

6. What were the two different ways that Harriet and Stuart reacted to the broken canoe?

   _____

   _____

7. How might the story have ended differently if Stuart had taken Harriet's suggestions?

   _____

   _____

   _____

8. Where did Stuart tell the lineman that Margalo was from?

   _____

   _____

9. Do you think Stuart enjoyed his search for Margalo? Why or why not?

   _____

   _____

   _____

10. On the back of this paper, write a short episode telling what might have happened to Stuart next. Include an illustration under the story.

Building Ames' Crossing

In the first paragraphs of Chapter 13, author E. B. White gives a detailed description of the town of Ames' Crossing. Below are some cutouts of items that were mentioned in this description. Collect the materials below and construct a diorama of Ames' Crossing.

Materials: oaktag, glue, scissors, crayons, or colored pencils

Directions

1. First, color the pictures below as neatly and realistically as possible.

2. Cut the forms out carefully. Keep the tabs on each form.

3. Carefully paste your cutouts on a piece of oaktag. When they are thoroughly dry, cut out around the forms.

4. Using a flat piece of oaktag as your base, design the size of your town.

5. Fold the tabs backwards along the dotted lines and paste onto your oaktag base. Have all forms facing you.

6. Design any other buildings or landscapes to finish the town.

You may work in pairs or set the town on a table and have the entire class contribute.

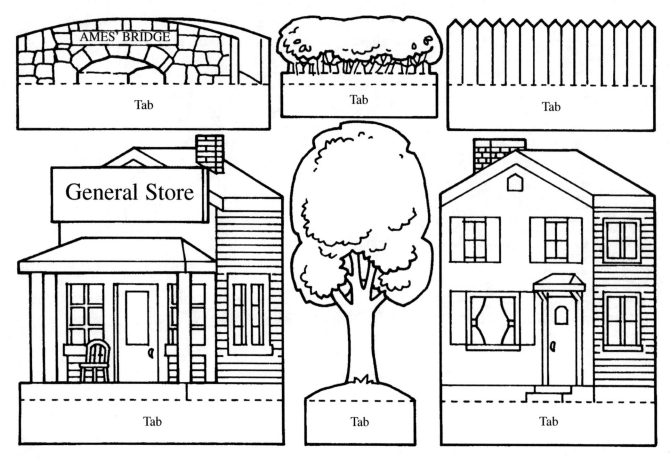

Flags and Messages

When Stuart was aboard his ship, the *Wasp*, he could have sent a message to the shore with flags. There is a special group of flags known as the international code of signals. Each letter of the alphabet has a special flag like the ones below. Using colored pencils, color each flag using these guide letters.

B = blue	**R = red**	**Bl = black**	**Y = yellow**	**W = white**

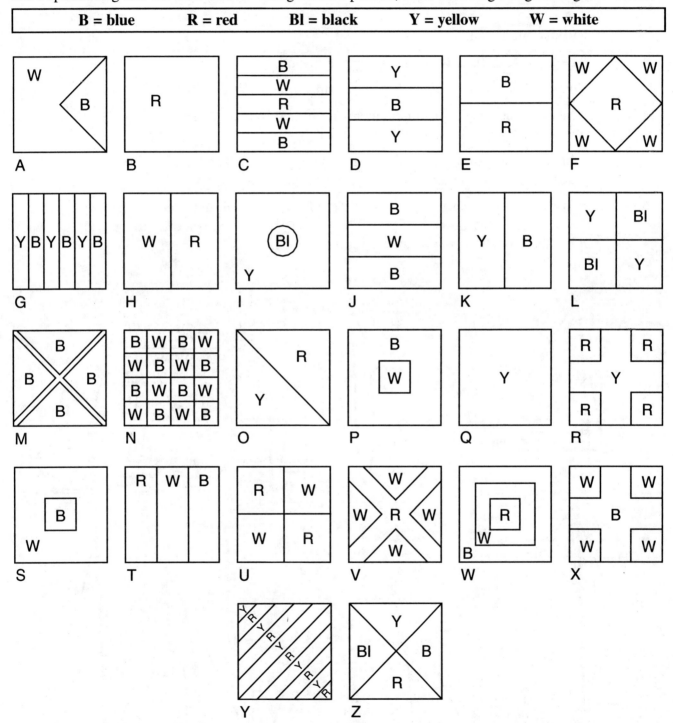

With a partner develop a short message using a paper towel roll for the handle and a sheet of 8½" x 11" (22 cm x 28 cm) paper to make the flags you need. Have the class read your message.

Sailboats

Stuart Little found sailing very exciting. Stuart sailed a type of sailboat called a *schooner*. There are many different types of sailboats. Below are descriptions of each type of sailboat drawn for you on this page. Match the type of sailboat with its description by writing the letter of the correct sailboat on the lines below.

1. _____ **catboat**—It has one main sail.

2. _____ **yawl**—It has three sails, each smaller than the other.

3. _____ **sloop**—This has two main sails. One is smaller and called a jib.

4. _____ **ketch**—A ketch has four sails. The main sail (tallest one) is located in the center and the two on the bow (front) are aligned together.

5. _____ **schooner**—Schooners have two main sails (large sails). The largest sail is in the stern (back). It has two smaller sails in the bow (front).

6. _____ **gaff cutter**—This has five sails. There is a large, wide sail in the center that reaches to the stern (back). It has a small, high sail that reaches from the main mast to the wide sail, and it has three small sails in the bow (front) of the boat.

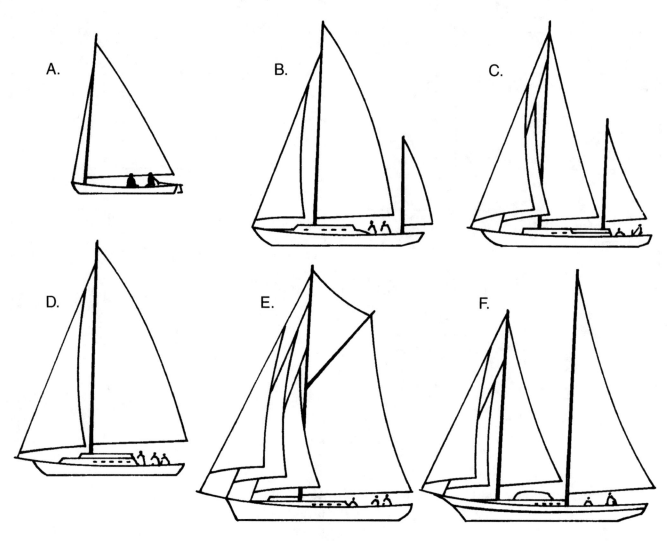

Choices

When Stuart and Harriet met to take a ride in Stuart's canoe, they reacted differently to finding the canoe damaged. Stuart was inconsolable over the loss. Harriet thought they could still have a nice time. She was an optimist, someone who looks on the bright side of things. Stuart was behaving like a pessimist, someone who sees the gloomy side of things.

Discuss with a classmate how the story might have changed had Stuart gone along with Harriet's suggestion.

To see how you would react to a problem, look at the situations below. Read each situation with two of your classmates and write your response to each question. Have them judge whether your response would be that of an optimist, who looks on the bright side, or a pessimist, who looks on the gloomy side of a situation. Have your classmates read your answers and check the box at the right.

What Would You Do?

	Optimist	Pessimist

1. Your mother promised to take you to an amusement park. It begins to rain heavily, and she tells you that you can't go today. What do you do?

   _____

   _____

   _____

2. You are picked for the basketball team. Tomorrow is your first game. You have an accident and fall off your bike and hurt your foot. You can't walk on your foot. What will you do tomorrow?

   _____

   _____

   _____

3. Last night you studied for a test in school today, but you studied the wrong pages! You take the test and get a poor grade. What would you do?

   _____

   _____

   _____

Any Questions?

When you finished reading *Stuart Little*, you may have had some questions that were not answered. Write them in the space below.

_____

_____

_____

_____

_____

_____

_____

Now, work in groups to answer your own questions or to prepare answers for the questions below. When you have finished, share your group's ideas with the class.

- Did Stuart ever find Margalo?

- How do you think the Little family felt after Stuart left?

- Was Stuart a mature person, or did he sometimes act in an immature way? Explain.

- What were some of the events in this story that you could call imaginary (fiction)?

- What would have happened if Stuart ever saw his family again?

- Name at least five acts of kindness you found in the book *Stuart Little*.

- Why did Stuart say that Miss Gunderson was sick because she had vitamin trouble?

- What do you think Harriet thought of Stuart?

- Why did Snowbell say he couldn't harm Margalo because she was a guest?

- Why was New York City a good setting for this story?

- How did Stuart show courage in the boat race in Central Park?

- Why do you think George never finished a project on which he worked?

- In what ways was Stuart clever?

- What part of Stuart's personality is like yours?

- How can you tell if Margalo liked Stuart?

36

Book Report Ideas

There are a variety of ways to report on a book you have just read. After you have finished reading *Stuart Little,* decide which method of reporting you would enjoy doing. You may use your own idea, or you may choose one of the ideas below.

Twenty Questions

After the class finishes the book, each student wears a sign on his or her back with the name of one of the characters from the book. Provide student with 20 slips of paper with his or her initials on each one. The students may move about the room and ask yes or no questions about their characters. They may not ask direct questions like, "Am I a mouse?" if there is only one mouse in the story. For each question they must give away a slip of paper. At the end of the 20 questions, each one can guess which character he or she has. You may shorten the questions to 10 or less to fit the situation.

Newspaper Hats

Place two sheets of newspaper crossways on the desk. Roll the sides of the paper up on all sides so that you have formed a hat. Tape down the rolled newspaper so that it doesn't unravel. Cut out strips of paper and write a sentence on each one about the book you have just read. Either tape slips of paper to a string on the hat or tape them directly to the hat. Ask students to explain to the class how the sentences fit with the book they read.

Street Signs

On a large sheet of oaktag, outline several streets of a city using a ruler. Give each street the name of a character in the story. Use rolled paper and a slip of oaktag to make a street sign for your street. Stand each sign in place on the map using glue or clay. On the block next to the sign, print information about the character or glue on objects that reflect the character. Explain to the class how the objects or information relate to the story.

Quick and Easy Balloon Report

Blow up large balloons. With a marker, gently print a sentence about the book on each balloon. Make sure to cover a variety of sections. One balloon should have the title and author of the book on it. Tie all the balloons together for a balloon report for your class.

TV Time

Construct a picture frame out of cardboard, 24" x 24" (61 cm x 61 cm) and 3" (8 cm) wide along all sides. Write the dialogue from one scene in the book explaining a major part of the story. Students appear behind the frame, "screen," or to act out the scene while reading the lines of the characters.

Dice

Each student cuts out six 5" (13 cm) squares. On each square, the student writes a different quote from a character in the book. Tape all six sides together to form a cube. Using teams, roll the cube and explain the quote that comes up on top of the square.

Whaling in America

Many people, like the people in Central Park, enjoy sailing for fun. Many years ago in the United States, people used large sailing ships to hunt whales in the ocean. Divide the class into teams of three and see which team can find the most information about whales and whaling.

Use the library, your books, or a computer to find the answers to these questions about whales and whaling in the United States.

- Why were whales hunted?
- What are three towns in the United States that were known for whaling?
- What type of boats did sailors use to hunt whales?
- How long did sailors have to be out in the water on a whaling trip?
- How did the whalers catch and kill the whales?
- What equipment would you have needed if you were a whaler?
- When did whaling stop in the United States?
- Which type of whale is the largest?
- What are the measurements and weight of the largest type of whale?
- What are the flukes on a whale?
- How thick is the blubber on a whale?
- Why do whales have blubber?
- Where is the "spout" of a whale located, and for what is it used?
- Do whales have lungs?
- How long can a whale hold its breath?
- How do whales sing and speak to one another?
- How does a baby calf learn to swim?
- How many types of whales are there, and what are some of their names?
- How could you tell one whale from another?
- Which whales have teeth, and which whales do not?

Key: 1 inch = 1 foot

Using all of the information you have learned, choose one type of whale, create a drawing to scale, using one inch (2.54 cm) for each foot. Write or type the information you have gathered on the whale and whaling and display it on a wall or bulletin board.

Artist's Corner

Often artists paint a picture to remember something special. Using your memory or imagination, create a painting of an experience Stuart had in the story, or of an experience you think Stuart may have had after the book was finished.

Preparation

1. Outline in pencil first.
2. Make your drawing large enough to be able to paint it easily (like pictures in a coloring book).
3. Use watercolors or poster paints.
4. Every part of your picture should be covered in paint. (Remember to let portions of the paint dry completely before painting the adjoining sections.)
5. Remember to use newspaper or some kind of covering to keep your desk, the floor, and the table clean.

Use the suggestions below to get started thinking of an idea:

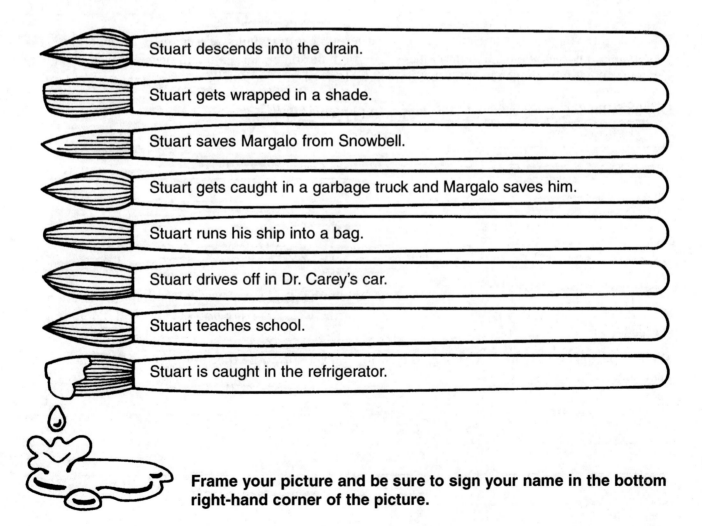

Stuart descends into the drain.

Stuart gets wrapped in a shade.

Stuart saves Margalo from Snowbell.

Stuart gets caught in a garbage truck and Margalo saves him.

Stuart runs his ship into a bag.

Stuart drives off in Dr. Carey's car.

Stuart teaches school.

Stuart is caught in the refrigerator.

Frame your picture and be sure to sign your name in the bottom right-hand corner of the picture.

Writer's Corner

The description of Ames' Crossing in the beginning of chapter 13 tells you about the setting of that chapter. Reread that section of chapter 13 aloud and then close your eyes to picture the scene. Writing a story is like drawing a picture with words.

Close your eyes and imagine how you would describe your room at home. Tell in detail what your bed looks like, where you keep your clothes, and where you keep your schoolbooks and toys. Is it neat and orderly or messy? What does the floor of your room look like? What sounds can you hear in your room? Can you smell dinner cooking? Do you feel safe, alone, happy, etc.?

On the following lines, describe your room.

_____

_____

_____

_____

_____

Now, imagine you are in your room and you hear a sound at the window. What does it sound like? Do you go and look? Do you call your mother? Do you hide somewhere in the room? Will you open the window? What will happen next? What do you feel, see, hear, and smell?

On the following lines, write what is happening in your room.

_____

_____

_____

_____

_____

What problem has been created? How do you deal with it? Are you clever in handling the situation? What do you do to make yourself feel safe, happy, or the way you felt before? How well did you succeed?

Write a paragraph about how you, as the main character, handle the situation to solve the problem.

_____

_____

_____

_____

_____

Create Your Own

E. B. White told the tale of *Stuart Little* in order, starting from Stuart's birth until his travels. A story usually has an order to it that can be easily understood, though not always believed. Below are parts of stories that make sense when put in order but are not always believable.

1. Cut out one part from each section and put them together to form a story. (You will have one from A, one from B, one from C, etc.)

2. Paste the parts together, in order, on a piece of paper.

3. Share the stories with your class.

A. Once upon a time, a young girl from the city sat quietly in a tree by a stream watching some geese.

A. Once upon a time, a tall redheaded boy sat by a stream tossing bread crumbs to two, large, honking geese.

A. Once upon a time, a teacher from our school sat by a roaring stream. Out of a bag the teacher took pieces of bread and tossed them to two, large, white geese, who darted and flapped as they dove for the crusty bread.

B. The young person grew tired in the warmth of the forest and lay down on a patch of moss and fell fast asleep.

B. One young goose grabbed the bag of bread crumbs and took off into the woods.

B. The largest of the geese spoke. "You are very kind," he said, "we would like to repay you. Sit on my back, and I will take you to a magical place."

C. Following the goose to deep within the forest, this person soon became lost.

C. Two geese, seeing the resting person and being thankful for the generosity shown to them, spread out their wings and shielded the sleeping person from the sun as it filtered through the trees.

C. The person saw the goose waiting and, grasping his shoulders, climbed aboard his back.

D. The goose flew through the air with the surprised person on his back. They flew past the sunset, the moon and stars, and into tomorrow.

Create Your Own *(cont.)*

D. They wandered about the forest for hours until the sun began to set.

D. A hunter came and, seeing the geese, lifted his bow and arrow to his shoulders and took aim at the beautiful creatures.

E. Before any harm could come to them, the loud frightening sound of a thunderstorm caused everyone to look up in fear.

E. Heading to the distant hill, they bravely came to rest at the foot of a large castle.

E. The person became frightened, knowing that they were lost.

F. Looking through a window, the girl or boy began tapping on the glass.

F. A great cloud came over all of them, and a voice spoke. "No harm comes to those who are kind in this forest."

F. Climbing to the top of a tree, he or she saw the lights of the city in the distance and knew it was the way home.

G. Reaching out, the youth captured three fireflies and, using them to light the way, returned safely home.

G. A light from the distance began to approach. Voices began to sing. Approaching, the girl or boy realized that the voices belonged to her or his parents who had been lost many years ago. They were all safely united and lived happily ever after.

G. She or He awoke with a start to see what was happening. The hunter's bow and arrow immediately turned to chocolate, which was shared by all.

Unit Test

Matching: Match the names of the characters to the best description of each one.

1. _____ Stuart   A. told the Angora cat how to catch Margalo

2. _____ Margalo   B. loved adventure

3. _____ Mrs. Little   C. was afraid Stuart would go down a mousehole

4. _____ Dr. Carey   D. was interested in places that Stuart went

5. _____ George   E. invited Stuart to her house for dinner

6. _____ Snowbell   F. sailed the *Lillian B. Womrath*

7. _____ Mr. Little   G. saved Stuart's life

8. _____ Harriet   H. never finished his projects

9. _____ LeRoy   I. Stuart's friend, a surgeon-dentist, owner of the schooner Wasp

True or False: Write True or False next to each statement below.

1. _____ The Little family was very kind to Stuart.

2. _____ Stuart won the boat race in Central Park easily.

3. _____ The pigeon saved Margalo's life.

4. _____ Stuart left home because he wanted a car.

5. _____ Stuart had a wonderful time with Harriet out on the river in his canoe.

6. _____ While he was on the road, Stuart made his car vanish to keep safe.

7. _____ Snowbell really liked Stuart.

8. _____ George was good to Stuart.

9. _____ Stuart was an intelligent mouse.

10. _____ The children at School #7 behaved badly.

Sequencing: Number the events below in the order they occurred in the story.

1. _____ Stuart leaves home to find Margalo.

2. _____ Mrs. Little loses her ring in the drain and Stuart finds it.

3. _____ Stuart Little wins the sailboat race.

4. _____ The window shade rolls up with Stuart inside it.

5. _____ Stuart meets Harriet, who is his size.

Essay

Being selfish means thinking only of yourself. Stuart behaved in both selfish and unselfish ways because he was young. On the back of this paper, write a two-paragraph essay about the ways that you would consider Stuart selfish and the ways you feel Stuart was unselfish.

Response

On a separate paper, explain the meaning of each of these quotations from *Stuart Little*.

Chapter 1:   *At birth Stuart could have been sent by first class mail for three cents, . . .*

Chapter 2:   *"I should feel badly to have my son grow up fearing that a farmer's wife was going to cut off his tail with a carving knife."*

Chapter 3:   *. . . and the other members of the household, dozing in their beds, would hear the bright sharp* plink plink plink *of Stuart's hammer . . . .*

Chapter 4:   *"I guess that will teach him to show off his muscles."*

Chapter 5:   *"If he is dead," said George, "we ought to pull down the shades all through the house."*

                    "As for my hat and cane being found at the entrance to the mousehole, you can draw your own conclusions."

Chapter 6:   *"Live and learn," muttered Stuart, tartly, putting his change purse back in his pocket.*

                    ". . . who doesn't understand sailing and who hardly knows a squall from a squid."

Chapter 7:   *"Watch out for flotsam dead ahead!"*

Chapter 8:   *"So!" thought Stuart. "I guess there's going to be something doing after all."*

Chapter 9:   *"What was it like, out there in the Atlantic Ocean?"*

Chapter 10:   *BEWARE OF A STRANGE CAT WHO WILL COME BY NIGHT.*

Chapter 11:   *"I ought to take along something to remember my mother by . . ."*

                    "Oh, mercy! Oh, mercy!" Stuart cried when he realized what he had done.

Chapter 12:   *"I'll make the work interesting and the discipline will take care of itself . . ."*

Chapter 13:   *"She's just your size . . . ."*

Chapter 14:   *. . . leaving Stuart alone with his broken dreams and his damaged canoe.*

(Note to Teacher: Choose the number of quotes for which you would like your students to respond.)

Conversations

Work in size-appropriate groups to write and perform the conversations that may have occurred in one of the following situations from *Stuart Little*.

- Mr. and Mrs. Little have a conversation about having someone so small for a son and what they must do to protect him.

- Stuart explains to his brother George what sailing across the pond in Central Park was like.

- Stuart tells Margalo what she should do to care for her sore throat.

- Margalo and Stuart discuss how they are going to get home from the garbage (scow) boat.

- The Angora cat and Snowbell talk about eating Margalo.

- Mr. Little tries to explain to the police that his son is missing.

- Dr. Carey, Stuart, and Mr. Clydesdale discuss Stuart's search for Margalo.

- The students at School #7 discuss with Stuart what is important to them.

- Stuart and Harriet talk about what they will do now that the canoe is destroyed.

- Stuart explains to the telephone pole man what Margalo is really like and why he must find her.

You may use the space below and the back of this sheet to write out your character's parts of the conversation.

_____

_____

_____

_____

_____

_____

_____

_____

_____

Bibliography of Related Reading

Fantasy

Cleary, Beverly. *The Mouse and the Motorcycle.* (W. Morrow, 1965)

Cleary, Beverly. *Ralph S. Mouse.* (W. Morrow, 1982)

Itse, Elizabeth. *Hey Bug! and Other Poems About Little Things.* (Heritage Press, 1979)

Jacques, Brian. *Martin the Warrior.* (Philomel Books, 1993)

Lawson, Robert. *Ben and Me.* (Little Brown, 1988)

Lawson, Robert. *Mr. Revere and I.* (Little Brown, 1988)

Weigelt, Udo. *The Strongest Mouse in the World.* (North South Books, 1998)

White, E. B. *Charlotte's Web.* (HarperCollins, 1999)

Mice

Bielfeld, Horst. *Mice.* (Barron, 1985)

Holmes, Kevin J. *Mice.* (Bridgestone Books, 1998)

Pfarr, Richard. *Mice as a New Pet.* (TFH Publishers, 1991)

New York City

Adams, Barbara Johnston. *New York City.* (Silver Burdett Press, 1988)

Biemer, Linda. *New York City.* (Gibbs Smith Publishers, 1994)

Brown, Richard. *A Kid's Guide to New York City.* (Harcourt Brace, 1988)

Doherty, Craig A. and Katherine M. Doherty. *The Statue of Liberty.* (Blackbirch, 1996)

Kerson, Adrian. *Terror in the Towers: Amazing Stories from the World Trade Center Disaster.* (Random Books Young Readers, 1993)

Mann, Elizabeth B. *The Brooklyn Bridge: The Story of the World's Most Famous Bridge and the Remarkable Family That Built It.* (Mikaya Press, 1996)

Pearlman, Carl J. *Take New York Home: The First 3-Dimensional Pop-up Map of New York.* (Multi Map, 1994)

Sailing

Bailey, Donna. *Sailing.* (Raintree Steck-Vaughn, 1990)

Barrett, Norman S. *Sailing.* (Watts, 1988)

Bayley, Thomas. *Sailing Ships: A Lift-the-Flap Discovery.* (Orchard Books Watts, 1998)

Braynard, Frank O. *Search for the Tall Ships.* (Braynard, 1986)

Henderson, Richard. *First Sail.* (Cornell Maritime, 1993)

McCurdy, Michael. *The Sailor's Alphabet.* (Houghton-Mifflin, 1998)

Small Boat Sailing. (Boy Scouts of America, 1995)

Visual Dictionary of Ships & Sailing. (DK Publishers, Inc., 1991)

Answer Key

Page 11

1. The size of Stuart's clothes and the size of his bed were problems.
2. Stuart had only gained ⅓ of an ounce after a month.
3. They made special clothing and bedding for Stuart and told him he was brave and didn't want him to hear anything bad about mice.
4. He was hardworking and pleasant. Accept all reasonable answers.
5. Stuart was not afraid. He went down the drain for the ring and went into the piano.
6. He could go down a drain, find Ping-Pong balls under things, go inside a piano, and enter mouseholes.
7. They didn't want him to hear "Three Blind Mice" and "The Night Before Christmas" as it was written.
8. Stuart exercised, put on his bathrobe, pulled the string for the light, and climbed up the sink to wash and brush his teeth.
9. George tried to construct a brace for Stuart so he could pry open the water faucet and had also promised to build a small washbasin.
10. Accept appropriate responses.

Page 13

Real: 1, 5, 8, 10, 12, 13, 17, 18, 19, 20
Fiction: 2, 3, 4, 6, 7, 9, 11, 14, 15, 16.

Page 16

1. He was showing off his muscles to Snowbell.
2. He said, "Holy mackerel!, I guess that will teach him to show off his muscles."
3. He put Stuart's hat and cane by the mousehole so they would think Stuart was down the hole.
4. He wanted to rip up the floor.
5. George pulled down the shade.
6. Someone in the house must have moved them there to mislead the others.
7. The dime was ½ his size.
8. Terms he used were: berth, jib, jibe, luff, leech, deck, dock, mast, aye, aye sir, ready about, and yawing.
9. It was a breezy day that drew Stuart to the park to go sailing.
10. He felt comfortable taking a bus, and he took over a ship he had never been on.

Page 17

A. sail	C. tiller	E. rudder	G. hull	I. jib	K. spar
B. boom	D. stern	F. keel	H. bow	J. rigging	

Page 18

1. E, 2. G/I, 3. B, 4. G/I, 5. A, 6. J, 7. C, 8. F, 9. H, 10. D

Page 21

1. He was a fat boy of 12 who wore a blue serge suit and a white necktie. He was sulky and wanted Stuart to be on his boat.
2. A policeman fell in the pond and created a wave that swept over the ships.
3. The officer fell in the pond. Stuart sailed into a bag. The Wasp had a collision. Stuart won the race.
4. She made him hot broth and put him to bed with a doll's hot water bottle at his feet.
5. Mrs. Little played tick-tack-toe with him, George made a soap bubble pipe and a bow and arrow, and Mr. Little made a pair of ice skates out of paper clips.

Answer Key *(cont.)*

Page 21 *(cont.)*

6. He offered her gargle, nose drops, *Kleenex*, and a thermometer.
7. Snowbell was going to eat Margalo.
8. She had followed him from the house and carried him home.
9. She made a tiny cake with seeds sprinkled on top.
10. Accept reasonable responses.

Page 26

1. The Angora cat was not a good influence on Snowbell because he told Snowbell he should eat the bird.
2. Accept all reasonable answers.
3. She was frightened and could not eat.
4. Accept all reasonable responses.
5. Stuart took his toothbrush, money, soap, comb, brush, underwear, and compass.
6. The dentist was working on his teeth.
7. Accept all reasonable responses.
8. He would make the work interesting, and the discipline would take care of itself.
9. He discussed what is important—laws and fairness.
10. Accept all reasonable responses.

Page 31

1. He should meet Harriet Ames because she was small, too.
2. The town may have been started by the Ames family, or they may have owned much of it. Any other reasonable response is acceptable.
3. The canoe probably leaked, and the storekeeper did not want to admit it.
4. Accept all reasonable responses.
5. It may not have been delivered.
6. Harriet wanted to fix it up and go anyway, but Stuart was heartbroken.
7. Accept any reasonable answer.
8. She was from fields, wheat, pastures, fern, and thistle.
9. Accept any reasonable response.
10. Accept any reasonable response.

Page 34

1. A, 2. B, 3. D, 4. C, 5. F, 6. E

Page 43

Matching: 1. B, 2. G, 3. C, 4. I, 5. H, 6. A, 7. D, 8. E, 9. F
True or False: 1. T, 2. F, 3. T, 4. F, 5. F, 6. F, 7. F, 8. T, 9. T, 10. F
Sequencing: 4, 1, 3, 2, 5
Essay: Accept all reasonable responses.

Page 44

Accept all reasonable responses.

Page 45

Perform the conversations in class. Discuss with the class whether these would be likely things the characters would say. Were the speakers convincing?

48